Nine
Fruits
of the
Spirit

A Bible Study on Developing Christian Character

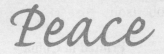

Peace

Robert Strand

New Leaf Press
A Division of New Leaf Publishing Group

First printing: June 1999
Third printing: September 2009

ISBN-13: 978-0-89221-463-1
ISBN-10: 0-89221-463-5
Library of Congress Number: 99-64009

Cover by Janell Robertson

Printed in China

Please visit our website for other great titles:
www.newleafpress.net

For information regarding author interviews, please contact the
publicity department at (870) 438-5288.

Contents

Introduction

There is an ancient story out of the Middle East which tells of three merchants crossing the desert. They were traveling at night in the darkness to avoid the heat of the day. As they were crossing over a dry creek bed, a loud attention-demanding voice out of the darkness commanded them to stop. They were then ordered to get down off their camels, stoop down and pick up pebbles from the creek bed, and put them into their pockets.

Immediately after doing as they had been commanded, they were then told to leave that place and continue until dawn before they stopped to set up camp. This mysterious voice told them that in the morning they would be both sad and happy. Understandably shaken, they obeyed the voice and traveled on through the rest of the night without stopping. When morning dawned, these three merchants anxiously looked into their pockets. Instead of finding the pebbles as expected, there were precious jewels! And, they were both happy and sad. Happy that they had picked up some of the pebbles, but sad because they hadn't gathered more when they had the opportunity.

This fable expresses how many of us feel about the treasures of God's Word. There is coming a day when we will be thrilled because we have absorbed as much as we have, but sad because we had not gleaned much more. Jewels are best shown off when held up to a bright light and slowly turned so that each polished facet can catch and reflect the light.

Each of these nine jewels of character will be examined in the light of God's Word and how best to allow them to be developed in the individual life. That is how I feel about the following three verses from Paul's writings which challenge us with what their Christian character or personality should look like. Jesus Christ has boiled down a Christian's responsibility to two succinct commands: Love the Lord your God with all your heart, mind, soul, and body, and love your neighbor like yourself. Likewise, Paul the apostle has captured for us the Christian personality in nine traits:

> But the fruit of the Spirit is love, joy, peace, patience, kindness, goodness, faithfulness, gentleness, and self-control. Against such things there is no law. Those who belong to Christ Jesus have crucified the sinful nature with its passions and desires. Since we live by the Spirit, let us keep in step with the Spirit (Gal. 5:22–25).

At the very beginning of this study, I must point out a subtle, yet obvious, distinction. The "fruit" of the Spirit is a composite description of what the Christian lifestyle and character traits are all about — an unbroken whole. We can't pick only the fruit we like.

Unlocked in these nine portraits are the riches of a Christ-centered personality. The thrill of the search is ahead of us!

Peace

EIRENE (Greek), pronounced I-ray-nay,
meaning: peace, prosperity,
quietness, rest, or to be set at
one with yourself again.

*THE FRUIT OF THE
SPIRIT IS . . . PEACE*

There are all kinds of peace in our world. There is the peace of death, the peace of Tibet where a nation has been conquered by a neighboring country, the peace of the tranquilizer at work, the peace where one partner has withdrawn into a shell out of self-preservation, the outward peace of a nation where a dictator rules with an iron hand, and the peace of an alcohol or drug-induced stupor. We have lots of kinds of peace — induced, artificial, and temporary. The poet Longfellow may have felt the same thing as he penned these words:

> And in despair I bowed my head;
> "There is no peace on earth," I said,
> "For hate is strong
> And mocks the song
> Of peace on earth, good will to men!"

Maybe we have reason to despair when a historian has pointed out that about 85 percent of all human history concerns itself with war and conflict — personal, national, or worldwide. But into this cynical, weary, war-torn, strife-filled world there is a positive message in regards to peace and the author of peace: "For unto us a child is born, to us a son is given, and the government will be on his shoulders. And he will be called Wonderful Counselor, Mighty God, Everlasting Father, PRINCE OF PEACE" (Isa. 9:6)! This theme of peace marks the life and ministry of the Prince of Peace. And I believe that without doubting, this prophetic verse points only to one person — Jesus Christ! The angels carried this theme when announcing his birth: "Glory to God in the highest, and on earth PEACE to men on whom his favor rests" (Luke 2:14).

But when Jesus began his ministry he must have thrown his followers off track with a jarring thought. They had been awaiting the fulfillment of the prophesies of peace and being set free from Roman rule. Jesus said, "Do not suppose that I have come to bring peace to the earth, I did not come to bring peace, but a sword. For I have come to turn a man against his father, a daughter against her mother, a daughter-in-law against her mother-in-law — a man's enemies will be the members of his own household" (Matt. 10:34–36).

To the casual reader it smacks of contradiction. To people with a superficial understanding of what peace is all about it is the opposite of what had been prophesied. However, upon deeper thought and research, there is a key to unlock the concept. Before real, true, deep peace can come into the life

Peacemakers who sow in peace raise a harvest of righteousness (James 3:18).

of an individual there must first be an uprooting, a pulling down, a throwing out of the old false gods; changing of attitudes; and the serving of a new Master. And Jesus predicted that this process could cause problems.

Jesus taught a lot about this subject by saying you don't sew a new piece of cloth on an old garment, nor do you place new wine into old wineskins that have dried up. Before peace can come there must be a complete change of character through the process He called a "new birth." Nobody can serve two masters — a fountain cannot give out both bitter and sweet water, a tree cannot produce good and bad fruit, light and darkness are incompatible, there is no fellowship between righteousness and unrighteousness.

So Christ starts at the point of need — cleans out the past and builds a new future with the proper attitudes in place which then lends itself to a new peaceful future! There will be peace in each and every individual's heart who has had a personal encounter with the Savior. And ultimately there will be no total peace on this earth until the Prince of Peace returns — then this world will experience this peace in a total way. James reminds us that "Peacemakers who sow in peace raise a harvest of righteousness" (James 3:18). Paul says, "The fruit of the Spirit is peace!"

This peace that Christ gives is not only in good circumstances of life, but it is a deep, abiding, inner tranquillity in all kinds of life circumstances. This is a peace that transcends troubles and turmoil — this is the peace of the fruit of the Spirit.

A friend visited an elderly woman badly crippled by arthritis, and asked her, "Do you suffer much?"

She responded, "Yes, but there is no nail here," and she pointed to her hand. "He had the nails, I have the peace." She pointed to her head. "There are no thorns here. He had the thorns, I have the peace." She touched her side, "There is no spear here. He had the spear, I have the peace." (Ralph Turnbull)

JESUS CHRIST IS OUR PEACE

For our first study on peace, begin by reading Ephesians 2:11–22.

Based on verse 11, why do people seem to need to make differences between the "us" group and the "them" group?

_____

_____

_____

_____

To whom is this letter addressed? Jews? Gentiles? The Church?

_____

_____

What do you think is wrong with "labeling" people?

_____

_____

_____

_____

Was there a problem in the Early Church between the Gentile believers and the Jewish believers? If so, describe it based on this Scripture portion:

_____

_____

_____

_____

_____

Is there a problem in our world with separate groups?

_____

_____

_____

_____

What can we do to overcome such barriers?

_____

_____

_____

_____

What did Jesus do to end such barriers and the resulting hostilities?

_____

_____

_____

_____

What part does peace play in ending separations?

_____

_____

_____

_____

_____

What are we to become (verse 19) and what are the implications?

_____

_____

_____

_____

_____

To whom did Jesus come to preach peace?

_____

_____

If Jesus came to do away with barriers of race, social status, gender, or ethnicity, why are so many of our churches divided over these issues?

_____

_____

_____

_____

Paul uses the analogy of God's people being "built" or constructed as a temple. In what way are you still under construction?

_____

_____

_____

_____

Before we leave this portion of God's Word, let's read again the last verse. "And in him you too are being built together to become a dwelling in which God lives by his Spirit" (Eph. 2:22). What an absolutely awesome thought — we are being built to become a dwelling for God! And that, in the final analysis, is what the fruit of the Spirit is all about.

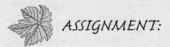 *ASSIGNMENT:*

• Let's take a moment to reflect on the above. Is prejudice still a problem with you? If so, how do you plan to deal with this life issue?

_____

_____

_____

• What positive steps can be taken to overcome prejudice or other barriers so that the peace of God can rule in your life?

_____

_____

_____

Personally?

_____

_____

_____

In your family?

_____

_____

_____

_____

In your church?

_____

_____

_____

_____

In your community?

_____

_____

_____

_____

PEACE WITH GOD

This element of the harvest of peace through the Spirit of God must be a deep, settled peace with God! This is our real possibility only through the blood of Jesus Christ which was shed. "But he was pierced for our transgressions, he was crushed for our iniquities; the punishment that brought us PEACE was upon him, and by his wounds we are healed" (Isa. 53:5). The guilty soul and conscience can only find peace by being made right with God through the sacrifice of Jesus Christ, God's Son. "For God was pleased to have all his fullness dwell in him, and through him to reconcile to himself all things, whether things on earth or things in heaven, by making peace through his blood, shed on the cross" (Col. 1:19–20). We are touching on a key element in experiencing peace in the individual soul. Without a peace with God there is no peace of God or any other kind of lasting peace.

We are dealing with the foundational truth upon which a life of fruit bearing is built — peace with God! This peace is the calm of sins forgiven. Read this verse once more and rejoice as you read it: "Therefore, since we have been justified through faith, WE HAVE PEACE WITH GOD through our Lord Jesus Christ" (Rom. 5:1). This is foundational and fundamental. To experience this peace with God lays the foundation for the peaceful conditions of a normal healthy body and mind. This peace is the product of the work of the Spirit within. It begins with a new birth. This peace is planted at this moment to be watered and nurtured and cultivated by the work of the Spirit in the individual believer's person. It's a process. This is a kind of "first-fruit" of the harvest of the Spirit.

There are a lot of people who believe they have the right prescription for peace, but we have just read about that perfect plan. Dominic Sarabia of Downey, California, collects autographs. That's not particularly remarkable, but his method of getting them is. He writes to high-profile people requesting their prescriptions for peace. Here are just a few from his extensive collection:

> Mother Theresa: "If we love each other as God loves each one of us, there will be peace. To be able to love as He loves, we need a clean heart — a heart free of all that is not love."

The guilty soul and conscience can only find peace by being made right with God through the sacrifice of Jesus Christ, God's Son.

Charles Manson: "Relax. Be now. You are the world as each is the world. Peace is within you. Come to one world for peace in life. The lines have been drawn in the universal mind." (Under this, Manson drew swastikas!)

G. Gordon Liddy: "If you want peace, prepare for war."

The late Isaac Asimov: "I don't have a prescription for peace I'm afraid, except that I'm pretty sure Christianity doesn't help."

Horror storywriter Stephen King: "My prescription for peace? Die. There's none to be had on this earth. Maybe that sounds grim. I don't mean it that way; there's a lot of sweetness in the world, but some guy is always gonna want to punch your nose — or maybe you'll want to punch his."

Fred (Mister) Rogers: "I think that peace begins with a sense of inner peace, and I firmly believe that comes from knowing that we are loved by the people who mean the most to us."

Pretty bleak answers, don't you agree? Until or unless we go to the Bible and to the Prince of Peace, there are no real answers to experiencing peace in this world. There is only one way and through one Person and His shed blood that any of us can find that peace with God!

S.D. Gordon wrote:

> When the heart's wrong, there can't be peace. Selfishness is a gangrene, eating at the very vitals. Sin is a cancer poisoning the blood. Peace is the rhythm of our wills with Jesus' love-will. Disobedience breaks the music. Failure to keep in touch makes discord. The notes jar and grate. We have broken off. The peace can't get in. Jesus made peace by his blood. We get it only by keeping in full touch with him.

For this study read Romans 5:1–11; 12:9–21.

When was the last time you really felt at peace and why did you feel that way?

_____

_____

_____

Based on our Bible reading, what does it mean to have peace "with" God?

_____

_____

_____

What are the things we are to rejoice in?

_____

_____

_____

How is it possible to have "peace with God"?

_____

_____

_____

_____

What do the following have to do with experiencing peace with God? Sufferings?

_____

_____

_____

_____

Perseverance?

_____

_____

_____

_____

Character?

_____

_____

_____

_____

Hope?

_____

_____

_____

_____

Explain the work of the Holy Spirit in producing hope:

_____

_____

_____

_____

What was the ultimate demonstration of love for us?

_____

_____

_____

_____

The word "reconciled" is used in verse 10. What does it mean?

_____

_____

_____

What is the cause for rejoicing?

_____

_____

_____

_____

Let's turn our attention to Romans 12:9–21. What does this portion of Scripture have to do with experiencing peace with God?

_____

_____

_____

_____

This portion deals with the how-to of peace — "If it is possible, as far as it depends on you, live at peace with everyone" (Rom. 12:18). Okay, explain how this should be done:

_____

_____

_____

_____

_____

_____

How would taking revenge destroy peace with God?

_____

_____

_____

_____

_____

_____

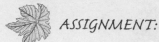

ASSIGNMENT:

• Are you currently experiencing "peace with God"? If not, write out the steps you can take to have that peace:

_____

_____

_____

_____

• What things prevent you from living in harmony with others?

_____

_____

_____

And what do you plan to do to restore any broken relationships to begin living in harmony with them?

_____

_____

_____

THE PEACE OF THE CHRISTIAN

Many stories have come to us out of the first century New Testament church about martyrdom. One such is about a particular Christian who had been sentenced to be burned at the stake. When the jailer came to get him out of his jail cell, he asked, "Are you upset and nervous about what will happen to you?"

To which the victim said, "Just place your hand over my heart and discover how calm I am."

The peace of the Christian is one of the themes that underlay much of what is written in the New Testament. It's almost an assumption that is unstated. This peace was the result of a promise Jesus made before He was taken away from them: "Peace I leave with you; MY PEACE I GIVE YOU. I do not give to you as the world gives. Do not let your hearts be troubled and do not be afraid" (John 14:27). And what a promise for our day and times. As a result of His peace, we are not to allow fear to grip us in our thinking or doing. His peace is the perfect antidote to troubled times! It's amazing how often this peace has been the theme of some of the best-loved hymns of the church.

Pardon a personal experience. It happened in Mankato, Minnesota, the first church I pastored. It was springtime, the winter had been long and hard with lots of snow on the ground. During the thaw, unseasonably warm spring rains fell, lots of rain combined with the run-off, and the rivers began to rise. There are a number of rivers that converge in or near the town — the Minnesota River being the largest. Levees had been built, sandbagging began, the town of North Mankato, where we happened to live, was evacuated. I took my three children and wife to my parents' home in Minneapolis and returned to help with the evacuation and sandbagging. The levee broke on the Mankato side, flooding a good portion of the town. We had a number of families who fled to the church for shelter and stayed there during the duration of high water.

The point of interest came on a Sunday morning, as we were returning from Minneapolis to conduct Sunday services. As we were stopped at the checkpoint by the National Guard, the officer asked my purpose in wanting back in. I simply said, "Sir, I am a pastor of the church and it's Sunday morning. Time for church."

He replied, "Reverend, it had better be a good one, because people will need all the help they can get."

Peace I leave with you; my peace I give you (John 14:27).

It was one of the most moving services I have ever been a part of. Seven or eight of our church families had already been flooded out and many others were in danger of their homes being inundated by flood, including our own. As the congregation sang the following hymn, I didn't observe a dry eye among us — some were singing with a hymnal in one hand and a handkerchief in the other:

What a treasure I have in this wonderful peace,
Buried deep in the heart of my soul,
So secure that no power can mine it away
While the years of eternity roll.

I am resting tonight in this wonderful peace,
Resting sweetly in Jesus' control;
For I'm kept from all danger by night and by day,
And His glory is flooding my soul.

Then the chorus:
Peace! Peace! Wonderful Peace,
Coming down from the Father above!
Sweep over my spirit forever, I pray,
In fathomless billows of love.
                    (W.D. Cornell & W.G. Cooper)

This peace of the Christian is a wonderful antidote to worries. This peace was demonstrated to us by Christ, untroubled in the face of a storm, sound asleep in the lower part of the ship while the 12 were scared to death. Twelve were worried while 1 was at rest. Do we see the same kind of ratio at work today? When the sea of life becomes turbulent — 12 will fret, worry, fume, and lose sleep while there is 1 among them who has learned to trust in that inner peace, who believes God, who will sleep and awake refreshed for another new day. Circumstances should never dictate nor produce peace or lack of peace. Christ is our source and that source is consistent no matter what may be happening all around us.

For this study our text will be taken from Philippians 4:1–13.

Again — what are the circumstances under which this letter was being written?

_____

_____

_____

_____

_____

Speculate — what was it that caused Euodia and Syntyche to be living in a situation which was anything but peaceful? What was it that had taken away their peace?

_____

_____

_____

_____

What kind of help can you offer to two friends who might be at odds with each other?

_____

_____

_____

To what is Paul referring when he mentions the "book of life"?

_____

_____

_____

What are the causes for rejoicing here?

_____

_____

_____

_____

Verse 6 takes us to the very core of this chapter — what does it mean to be anxious?

_____

_____

_____

What does "gentleness" have to do with peace?

_____

_____

_____

_____

Paul gives us a simple formula which allows the peace of God to do its work in our spirits. What do you think he means with the following terms?

Prayer?

_____

_____

Petition?

_____

_____

Thanksgiving?

_____

_____

Present?

_____

_____

Requests?

_____

_____

What do you think is the connection between the peace of God guarding our heart and mind in verse 7 and the directions given in verse 8?

_____

_____

_____

_____

What role does your thinking and attitude have in living a peaceful life?

_____

_____

_____

_____

Is there another secret to living in peace from verses 11–13? If your answer is "yes," please explain:

_____

_____

_____

What are the implications of verse 13 to you today?

_____

_____

_____

 ASSIGNMENT:

• When you were growing up, what were the elements that made you feel safe and secure?

_____

_____

_____

• Are you currently living with that peace of God in your life? If not, what do you plan to do to recapture that lost peace?

_____

_____

_____

_____

BRINGING PEACE INTO YOUR CURRENT LIFESTYLE

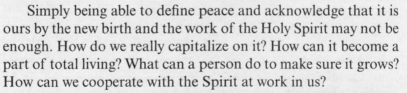

Simply being able to define peace and acknowledge that it is ours by the new birth and the work of the Holy Spirit may not be enough. How do we really capitalize on it? How can it become a part of total living? What can a person do to make sure it grows? How can we cooperate with the Spirit at work in us?

By loving His law: The Psalmist, whose own personal life had experienced a few ups and downs of life penned these words centuries ago: "Great peace have they who love your law, and nothing can make them stumble" (Ps. 119:165). It's so easy to-day to consider the Bible as being out of date and irrelevant to modern-day living. However, it is the inspired wisdom of the ages

The word rule *means to "preside," or more literally, to "arbitrate." The origin of the word is from the Greek and taken from what an umpire would do at any Grecian athletic game. It's a calling of the shots, in our vernacular. We are making the choices about the peace of God as applied to specific situations. Other translations read like this: "Let the peace of God rule in your hearts" (AV), or as Weymouth translates it, "Let the peace which Christ gives settle all questionings."*

as penned under the direction of the Spirit of God at work in a writer's life. How foolish to ignore it! Here are the keys to life, to living in peace with God, your fellow persons, and yourself.

Dr. Smiley Blanton, director of the American Foundation of Religion and Psychiatry, was asked if he read the Bible. His answer: "I not only read it, I study it. It's the greatest textbook on human behavior ever put together. If people would just absorb its message, a lot of us psychiatrists could close our offices and go fishing."

Among the things God's Word does is that it sets basic principles for peace in the human heart: "underneath are the everlasting arms — love your neighbor as yourself — take no thoughts about tomorrow — you shall know the truth and the truth shall set you free — don't be afraid — great peace have the people who trust in their God" — and a whole lot more! The Bible is the handbook on peace — become familiar with it. As we read it, we become aware of a whole lot of people who were just like us with the same kinds of problems, but because of the peace they found they were able to overcome the obstacles of this life!

Practice peace: To have the peace of God ruling our minds and spirits we must put to practice some of the principles of peace. It's not all 100 percent on the part of the Spirit. We have a role to play in developing this harvest of fruit. "Let [YOU let] the peace of Christ rule in your hearts, since as members of one body you were called to peace. And be thankful. Let the word of Christ dwell in you richly as you teach and admonish one another with all wisdom" (Col. 3:15–16).

William James, philosopher/psychologist, earlier in this century had a lot to say about this scriptural injunction: "The person who has daily inured himself to habits of concentrated attention, energetic volition and self-denial will stand like a tower when everything rocks about him and when his softer fellow mortals are winnowed like chaff in the blast. Sow an action and you reap a habit; sow a habit and you reap a character; sow a character and you reap a destiny."

Peace can come into our hearts by letting it rule in our minds and actions. This was the peace of mind, heart, and character which Jesus always exhibited in His life on this earth. This was especially evident during the trying hours of the ordeal of the trial and crucifixion. He set the example! He is the pattern! We are to let, grant permission, allow, condone, approve, authorize, and consent to allow the peace of God to work in our living!   .

When H.B. Macartney, an Australian pastor, visited Hudson Taylor in China, he was amazed at the missionary's serenity in spite of his many burdens and his busy schedule. Macartney finally mustered up the courage to say, "You are occupied with millions, I with tens. Your letters are pressingly important, mine of comparatively little value. Yet I am worried and distressed while you are always calm. Tell me, what is the difference?"

Taylor replied, "I could not possibly get through the work I have to do without the peace of God which passes all understanding keeping my heart and mind."

Macartney later wrote, "He was in God all the time, and God was in him. It was the true abiding spoken of in John 15."

For this study, read Psalm 46 and 91.

Based on your reading of these two Psalms, what is the relationship between experiencing the peace of God and trusting God?

_____

_____

_____

If we are to "let" the peace of God rule in our daily lives, how is the best way to start this exercise?

_____

_____

_____

_____

What do you think about when you read Psalm 46:1?

_____

_____

_____

What are your greatest fears?

_____

_____

_____

_____

Can you find the answer to them in either of these Psalms? If you have the antidote to your fears, write it down:

_____

_____

_____

God is described as being a "fortress." Why were fortresses built and for what purposes?

_____

_____

_____

What are the "works" that God is willing to do in your personal life?

_____

_____

_____

_____

From Psalm 91, what images come to your mind in regard to God's protection and care?

_____

_____

_____

_____

From Psalm 91, what are the specific dangers the writer uses to illustrate God's protective, loving care of His own?

_____

_____

_____

Are there counterparts in our modern world? Explain:

_____

_____

_____

_____

Explain the ministry of God's angels:

_____

_____

_____

_____

Do you really believe you have a guardian angel? If so, how would you explain this to an inquiring friend?

_____

_____

_____

_____

Have you ever had an "angel" minister to you? Have you ever sensed an angelic presence in your life?

_____

_____

_____

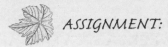 *ASSIGNMENT:*

• Are you presently experiencing any life situations which make you feel unsafe or vulnerable or upset?

_____

_____

_____

• How can you apply the principles of peace to your current situation?

_____

_____

_____

EVERLASTING PEACE

"Sarge" from the "Beetle Bailey" cartoon strip is shown in the first frame as having purchased some items at a store and as he's leaving the counter, the checkout lady says, "Thank you. Have a nice day."

> *The peace experienced here will sustain and keep us all the days of our life in the here and now as well as in the by and by.*

Sarge turns and asks, "Just a nice DAY? Why not a nice WEEK? A nice YEAR? A nice FOREVER? A nice. . . ."

At this point the checkout lady interrupts and says, "Look! Try to have a nice ten minutes, Okay?" (Mort Walker, Beetle Bailey)

Okay — how about having "peace" forever? We need more than a finite portion of peace — we need peace that lasts until the end of time! None of our studies, so far, has given us any indication as to how long the peace of God should last in the human soul. But it is implied that what has been given will last for eternity! The peace experienced here will sustain and keep us all the days of our life in the here and now as well as in the by and by. Jesus said "You did not choose me, but I chose you and appointed you to go and bear fruit — FRUIT THAT WILL LAST" (John 15:16). How long is that peace to last?

I cannot find any place in the Word where the peace was given for a specific period, then to be taken out of this world. This lasting aspect doesn't only apply to peace, but to all the fruits of the Spirit. We're dealing with eternity while still here in time.

Our next study will take us into heaven and eternity. Jesus is about to be crucified and taken away from His followers — lovingly, carefully, He prepares them for His absence. He speaks of heaven. By His words He leaves behind His peace, and promises to send them a Comforter to take His place. It's a poignant time, a parting, a last word and a last testament kind of time.

Last words seem to carry more of an impact and may be more important than what had preceded them — not that any of Christ's words were more important than any others. The words that He spoke were life and peace. I don't think the disciples realized what was happening nor what was about to happen. But in retrospect they were able to put it together and write about it, as John did, for all time, for all of us, today.

For our last study, begin by reading John 14:1–4, 15–27.

What frame of mind do you think the disciples had when Jesus shared those comforting words we have heard so often in verses 1–4?

_____

_____

_____

Where is the "Father's house" and what is it?

_____

_____

_____

_____

What will the prepared place be like?

_____

_____

_____

_____

To what was Jesus referring when He promised to return and "take you to be with me"?

_____

_____

_____

_____

Now to verse 15 — what do you see as the relationship between love, obedience, commands, and peace?

_____

_____

_____

Who is the "Counselor" and what is to be His function?

_____

_____

Jesus also promised not to leave them as "orphans," but promised to come to them. How does this happen?

_____

_____

How do we know that Jesus was doing the will of the Heavenly Father?

_____

_____

Describe in your own words the kind of "peace I leave with you" would be:

_____

_____

_____

Apparently there is a difference between the "peace I leave with you" and "my peace I give you." What is the difference between leaving it or giving it?

_____

_____

_____

What is so different about the peace He would give to us compared with the way "the world gives"?

_____

_____

_____

What does the phrase, "Do not let your hearts be troubled" really mean to you?

_____

_____

_____

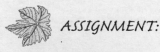 *ASSIGNMENT:*

• Are you presently at peace with yourself, your God, and your relationships?

_____

_____

If not, please write out a plan to have this peace restored where it is needed.

_____

_____

_____

• Think of one relationship which is not peaceful. How will you go about turning it into a peaceful relationship?

_____

_____

• And one more — what have you learned about yourself and about the peace of God through this study?

_____

_____

• How would you help someone else find peace with God?

_____

_____

IN SUMMARY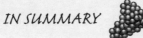

Henri Nouwen, a widely acclaimed author, educator, and Roman Catholic priest, tells how he came to a deeper understanding of peace, especially that peace which comes from God. In the 1980s, after having lived and taught at Harvard University, he moved to a community near Toronto called Daybreak — a "family" comprised of six mentally handicapped individuals and four who were not, all seeking to live by the beatitudes of Jesus.

In this life of mutual sharing, it has been Adam who has had the deepest impact on Nouwen. He is a 25-year-old man who cannot speak, cannot dress or undress himself, cannot walk alone, and cannot eat without much help. He does not cry or laugh. He suffers from severe epilepsy and, despite heavy medication, sees few days without grand mal seizures.

To many people Adam is a virtual "vegetable," but not to Nouwen: "As my fears gradually lessened, a love emerged in me so full of tender affection that most of my other tasks seemed boring and superficial compared with the hours spent with Adam. Out of his broken body and broken mind emerged a most beautiful human being offering me a greater gift than I would ever offer him."

Adam gave him the gift of peace — "a peace rooted in being." Nouwen had been caught up in his prestigious career — one "so marked by rivalry and competition, so pervaded with compulsion and obsession, so spotted with moments of suspicion, jealousy, resentment and revenge." But with Adam he discovered there was more to life and ministry. "Adam's peace, while rooted more in being than in doing, and more in the heart than in the mind, is a peace that calls forth community. Adam, in his total vulnerability, calls us together as a family."[1]

In this short series of studies, we have not nearly plunged into the depths of understanding peace and what it means to the Christian. But my hope is that your appetite has been stimulated to continue with this biblical study. How about doing a word study? Search through a concordance and look up every verse in which the word "peace" appears. It is a character commodity in very short supply today.

Let's read it again and again — until it's memorized, until the truth of this promise is driven deep into our needy souls:

> PEACE I leave with you; my PEACE I give you. I do not give to you as the world gives. Do not let your hearts be troubled and do not be afraid (John 14:27).

When the final history of this 20th century has been written, it could likely be said that this world during these 100 years has sought more and found much less peace than all the generations before us. It has been elusive even though this world has fought two different world wars to end all conflict and bring peace. Even as I write, even though the world is at present not at war, there are "civil" wars, "ethnic" cleansings, "racial" strife, and rebellions going on all over this globe.

If national or world peace has been elusive, then personal peace is just as elusive. People today are seeking peace by doing all kinds of things — most self-destructive. The search continually goes on in drunkenness, sexual excesses, drug-induced stupors, the self-intoxication of greed, and all the other fruitless pursuits of peace.

What an age and what a time for the voice of real, true, vital, peaceful Christianity to be sounded with a call so clear and so clarion that all this world may really see the Prince of Peace! What a day for the church to come forward and be counted! What a day for individuals to live out the peace that passes all understanding before a cynical and skeptical world! Yes! Peace can be had here and now and in this life!

What a call for Christians to act like Christians! What a day for the Church to be the Church! This world has had enough of phony, empty, fighting religion. Think of the impact we could have if — IF — we really were the people of peace!

Our challenge has been trumpeted by James:

> But the wisdom that comes from heaven is first of all pure; then PEACE — LOVING, considerate, submissive, full of mercy and good fruit, impartial and sincere. PEACEMAKERS who sow in peace raise a harvest of righteousness (James 3:17–18).

Think of the harvest of righteousness which could be unleashed when we go about sowing peace! When you sow, be careful, because you always reap more than you sow — which is to our advantage! It works in a positive sense as well as in a negative sense. Let's sow peace everywhere we go — sow it in the lives of others with whom we work and play and shop. This was the ministry of Jesus Christ as expressed by Paul, "He came and preached peace to you who were far away and peace to those who were near" (Eph. 2:17). There's our ministry, our pattern, and our challenge!

All of us who have experienced and been the recipients of His peace have a responsibility to those who are far away from peace as well as those who are near to peace! We have the tools — we have the know-how — we have the Word! Now it's up to us to just do it! Out of who we are and have become, we have the message of peace! Let's share it!

Only after we have achieved the peace of God can we join with Longfellow on his last verse of that famous Christmas carol:

> Then pealed the bells more loud and sweet
> "God is not dead nor doth He sleep.
> The wrong shall fail, The right prevail,
> **WITH PEACE ON EARTH,**
>   good will to men!"

John the Baptist's father was exultant, filled with the Holy Spirit and prophesied that "because of the tender mercy of our God by which the rising sun will come to us from heaven to shine on those living in darkness and in the shadow of death, TO GUIDE OUR FEET INTO THE PATH OF PEACE" (Luke 1:77–79).

What a prayer to pray: "LORD, GUIDE OUR FEET INTO THE PATH OF PEACE!"

Paul sent a wonderful, loving greeting to his dear friend and fellow worker, Philemon, which I would also like to send to you:

Grace to you and PEACE from God our Father
and the Lord Jesus Christ (Philem. 3).

And the fruit of the Spirit is . . . PEACE!

1   Henri Nouwen, "Adam's Peace," *World Vision*, August/September 1988, p. 4–7.

Robert Strand

Retired from a 40-year ministry career with the Assemblies of God, this "pastor's pastor" is adding to his reputation as a prolific author. The creator of the fabulously successful Moments to Give series (over one million in print), Strand travels extensively, gathering research for his books and mentoring pastors. He and his wife, Donna, live in Springfield, Missouri. They have four children.

Rev. Strand is a graduate of North Central Bible College with a degree in theology.

Nine Fruits of the Spirit

Study Series includes

Love • Joy • Peace • Patience • Kindness
Goodness • Faithfulness • Gentleness • Self-Control